The Key Elements of Trading Plan

Ahura Chalki

Copyright © 2012 Ahura Chalki

All rights reserved.

ISBN: **1725913461**
ISBN-13: 978-1725913462

DEDICATION

To my son, Joseph and my daughter Feren, my energies for work and life.

CONTENTS

Acknowledgments

1. What is Trading Plan?
2. Why we need to have Trading Plan?
3. Trading Plan Step 1: Emotion
4. Trading Plan Step 2: Find your trading session.
5. Trading Plan Step 3: Which Market are you interested in?
6. Trading Plan Step 4: Master your Markets!
7. Trading Plan Step 5: Risk Management.
8. Trading Plan Step 6: Set Goals.
9. Trading Plan Step 7: Set Exit Rules.
10. Trading Plan Step 8: Set Entry Rules.
11. Trading Plan Step 9: Keep records.
12. Recap – Time to Start!
13. About Author

ACKNOWLEDGMENTS

Thanks to all my employees in "Zero Spread" company who I a m really learning from them every day and strongly believe that they are the best in their professions with big future of success!

WHAT IS TRADING PLAN?

> A guideline for your trading activity, which covers every aspect of your trading system. - What supposed to be done, why, when & how!!

Trading also is like life, economic life. One of most common problem between people who are trading is that they do not look at that as a real business, they are just looking after special opportunity to get millions of dollars in one night. Here also like all other businesses you need to have guide line and follow that. Make a plan, how much you want to make monthly base, then weekly base and daily base. Once you reach your daily golf, get out of market, sit, put your hands on each other and just keep your eyes on that and follow the movement.

To better understanding I am **bringing** you an example:

Long term plan (Based on 15% monthly) profit

Starting Capital	expectation of profit 1th year	expectation of profit 2th year	expectation of profit 3th year	expectation of profit 4th year	expectation of profit 5th year
1000	1800				
2th Year Capital	2800	7840			
3th Year Capital		7840	21952		
4th Year Capital			21952	61465.6	
5th Year Capital				61465.6	172103.68

How to calculate
Capital x expected % of monthly income x 12 + capital

So now based on our long term plan, what we need to do is to create our short term plan, which is daily base, and based on our monthly expectation of profit. So, let's take first month as example, our expectation is 15% gross income, which is 1,800 USD and we have 22 trading days. 1800 divided 22 days, will give us almost 80 USD profit. So it is our daily plan and as soon as we catch the plan, the best thing is to get out of the market and wait for next trading day. Same as other months and days.

> **It is created based on your lifestyle, your interests/preferences and personality– Unique for every trader**

Second part of plan is working plan. We need to make a plan about the time which we want to use for trading. We can manage it based on our strategy, interest and working hours and so on, but make sure you will have special plan for that, as well and do not try mix it with something else and lose your focus.

WHY WE NEED TRADING PLAN?

- "FAIL TO PLAN AND YOU PLAN TO FAIL"
- Gives you Confidence on your Trades
- Keeps you focused on the process not the result (on planning and executing your strategy properly)
- Takes Emotions away - Creates Discipline
- Creates Consistency and Simplifies your trading
- Help you improved as a trader – Experience

TRADING PLAN STEP 1: EMOTION!

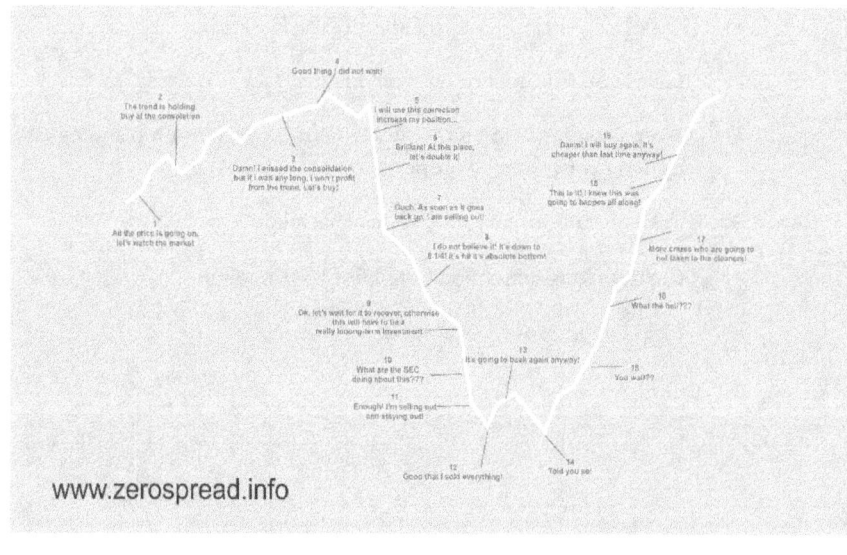

- Emotions – SOMETHING TO AVOID IN TRADING – Cause Irrational Decisions
- Don't trade if you are Angry, distracted by something else, psychologically down etc.
- Clean Mind is always the best advisor.

The Key Elements of Trading Plan

In trading which I can say 90% emotion is important, 5% since and 5% money management. About knowledge and money management we will talk later. Here what is important to know is that never enter to the market, while you are angry, upset, emotional, had a fight with your partner, boyfriend or girlfriend. Before everything first make sure you are emotional stable, happy and relax, then read the news, study the market and make decision. Most of traders are making great money, but what is making them to do not catch the aim is losing. I met a trader who was making money in seven positions, out of ten, but his biggest mistake was that in one negative trade, was losing twice more than all other seven positive trades. The reason was that he was not following the rolls, specially this topic which we are talking about. When he had 5-6 success positions, was becoming so emotional and for next trade could not make logical decision.

To be able to control your emotions in trading, of course you need experience, it is needed, but not enough! As much as you have more experience, you will be able to trade more calm and confidence, but it does not mean that if you have enough experience in trading, you will be able to trade in any situation, we are all human and in emotional situations, we do make more mistakes than normal situation. So always no matter if you are experienced trader or beginner, better to have some physical exercisement, cope of the coffee and check everything at least for 30 minutes before opening any position and then start. The reason of physical exercisement is because that your mind and manner to realize that they are going to be in new environment and feel the changes and become more focused.

TRADING PLAN STEP 2: FIND YOUR TRADING SESSION

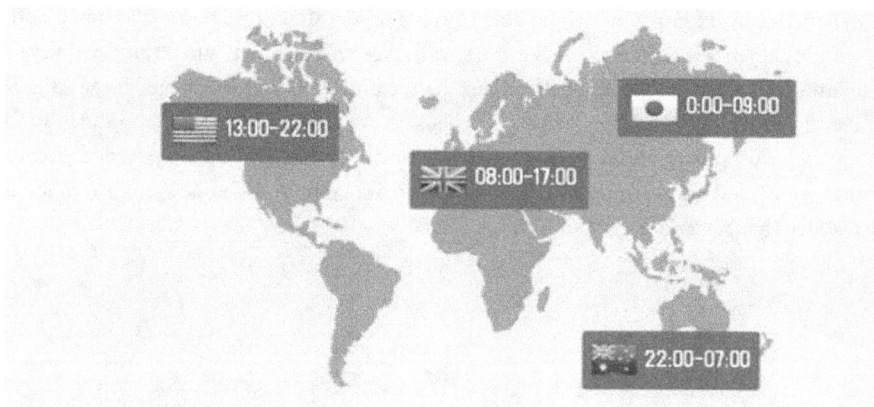

Important Questions:

- Is trading your permanent job?
- Is it something that you doing for extra income?
- What's your Daily time availability?
- In which markets am I interested in?
- What's their opening hours?
- Do they suit my Daily routine?
- What is your level of knowledge?
- It is better if you close all your positions by the end of your session – Go home Calm!

The Key Elements of Trading Plan

Like all other plans and things to do in your life, for trading also we need to know what do you need for, that? Is that something we want to base our life on? We want it as our premium job and income or secondary or for learning or...? As always we say, as long as you do not know where to go, you go nowhere, same as here in Trading, as long as you do not answer this question seems you are doing nothing and just wasting your time and money to do nothing and go nowhere, so please before doing anything, take a time, a paper and a pen and write down exactly why do you want that to do. Why it is important to write it down is because when we do write something, it makes us to think more and have better Ideas of what we are going to do!

Exactly now, right after that you realize what exactly you want from trading, now you can decide how long do you need per day to spend for that. Whole your day as premium job and income or secondary income after your main job? What time you can do that? Are you working day shift and can make it evenings after your work or working at nights and during day you do have time to spend for trading? It is important to know that, because based on answers of those questions you will be able to select the market you want to work on that and then start learning more about that exact market, like opening hours, special news which you need to follow for that and usually those news will be announced in which days and what times and so on. With knowing all those factors and knowing about the level of your knowledge in financial market and trading you will be able to choose which symbol(s) exactly you want trade with.

As much as important to answer all those questions, it is time to answer another important question, do you want to have short term positions? Long term? Do Scalping or...? They are all trading strategies. Yeah, you need to select your exact strategy which you want to have in your trade. Without having strategy it is really hard to trade or may can say impossible. If you want to have very short positions or doing scalping, so you will be able to close your positions every day in the end of your trading time (if you are doing as part time job) and next day, again new position. Or you may want to go for long term positions and during your trading time, follow the market just and learn more about that and have one or two positions for longer time, or waiting for special moments and opportunities to enter the market and keep the position for few weeks or months even.

TRADING PLAN STEP 3: WHICH MARKET ARE YOU INTERESTED IN?

- ➢ Decide in **which market are you interested in** – Currency, Stocks, Bonds, Commodities etc.
- ➢ Keep **few charts** on your screen – Keep it Simple!
- ➢ Find a **suitable Trading Timeframe**.
    - Depends on the your available time

The Key Elements of Trading Plan

- Personality

Decide in which market are you interested in – Currency, Stocks, Bonds, Commodities etc. Nobody can be perfect in all markets, so based on your knowledge and experience, focus on one market to get the best out of that. If you want to trade in other markets in same time, like currency and commodities (most famous markets) in this case at least you need to know the co-relations between them. However, here also other objections will come out, like which currencies, we have so many symbols here in market which you can choose them, like EURUSD, USDZAR, USACAD, etc. Any of those symbols depend on different news, political situation, geopolitical situation, financial news, different economic development or un-development and so on. So better to select few of them, which we can follow the important indexes about them and then we can find the correlation between them and some symbols in commodities, like what is the relation between Oil price and USDCAD or Gold with USDJPY and so on. So please before starting to trade in any of them, make sure you will be able to get enough information about them and you really like it as well. Once you are there and know already which symbols are suitable for you to trade, then next step is to open different windows in your MT4 or MT5 platform to see their movement and move to the next step.

TRADIMNG PLAN STEP 4: MASTER YOUR MARKETS

GMT	Time left		Event	Vol.	Actual	Consensus	Previous
			TUESDAY, SEP 05				
01:45	✓	CNY	Caixin China Services PMI (Aug)		52.7	51.8	51.5
04:30	✓	AUD	RBA Rate Statement REPORT				
04:30	✓	AUD	RBA Interest Rate Decision		1.5%	1.5%	1.5%
05:45	6m	CHF	Gross Domestic Product s.a. (QoQ) (Q2)			0.5%	0.3%
05:45	6m	CHF	Gross Domestic Product (YoY) (Q2)			1.1%	1.1%
07:15	1h 36m	CHF	Consumer Price Index (MoM) (Aug)			0.0%	-0.3%
07:15	1h 36m	CHF	Consumer Price Index (YoY) (Aug)			0.5%	0.3%
07:55	2h 16m	EUR	Markit PMI Composite (Aug)			55.7	55.7
07:55	2h 16m	EUR	Markit Services PMI (Aug)			53.4	53.4
08:00	2h 21m	EUR	Markit Services PMI (Aug)			54.9	54.9
08:00	2h 21m	EUR	Markit PMI Composite (Aug)			55.8	55.8
09:10	3h 31m	AUD	RBA's Governor Philip Lowe Speech SPEECH				
12:00	6h 21m	USD	FOMC Member Brainard Speech SPEECH				
14:00	8h 21m	USD	Factory Orders (MoM) (Jul)			-3.2%	3.0%
17:10	11h 31m	USD	FOMC Member Kashkari Speech SPEECH				
22:05	16h 26m	USD	FOMC Member Kaplan Speech SPEECH				

Please note that Server Time is subject to Daylight Savings Time (DST), which begins on the last Sunday of March and ends on the last Sunday of October.

Server Times:
Winter: GMT+2
Summer: GMT+3 (DST)

➤ **What you need to check before the Market Open**

- What's going on around the world?

- Determine what the **overall market sentiment** is for the day.

- Is the market that I am interested in affected?

- HOW? UP or down?

The Key Elements of Trading Plan

- What Economic data are due today?
- Will I trade ahead or after the data release?

No we are going to step in the market, almost there. Already we know what we want to trade with and our expectation from market. We know what time and how long we have time for that and ready to have our first trade. Now it is time to go to checking the information. First step here is to open the list of daily and weekly news to know what important news we have for this week and specially today. We have two options now:

- Analyze the market and based on guessing the results of news (forecast) and open the position.

- Waiting for results and then open the position.

However, all of them depend on your trading strategy, but for any strategy, you need to follow all the news related to your trading market.

What we need to remember is that it is not just economic news which is important, we have to have information about political news as well as technology related news in market.

TRADING PLAN STEP 5: RISK MANAGEMENT

% Loss of Capital	% Gain Required to Recover Loss
10%	11.11%
20%	25
30%	42.85
40%	66.66
50%	100
60%	150
70%	233
80%	400
90%	900
100%	Broke

> How much of your portfolio are you willing to risk Daily?
> Set **a Fixed % level** that you are willing to **risk per trade and per day.**
- E.g. 1% of your trading account per trade, or 5% of your Wallet per Day in total.
> *If this amount is lost, stay out of market for the rest of your Day!*
> Example: Account Equity: $5,000

The Key Elements of Trading Plan

Daily Risk: 5%

Daily Risk $$: $250 per Day. – **Maximum Daily loss permitted**

➢ Even If you trade more than 1 position trades, **STAY within your Risk limit.**

— E.g. 1% per trade.

4 Trades taken so if the overall risk hit **5% decline – Stop for the day! Tomorrow is a new day, with new opportunities.**

➢ Don't overtrade! **Set a maximum number of trades** you can make per day

➢ Don't more than 2 entries per idea – avoid double loss

➢ Helps you Avoid Impulse and Revenge trading - **Emotions**

It was just an example to understand how it works. Since we have plan for our profit, daily, monthly and yearly, we have to have a risking plan as well, which we call it risk management, as it is mentioned in first step that once you get your expected profit in a day, just step out of market and just follow the market for your rest of the day, it is same as for risking %, if you lost, do not be emotional and go again and start new position right after that, just step back, stay online and follow the market. I always give this example to be more clear, "never step in to new relation after you quite with your exe, just wait for better chance", make sure it works exactly same in financial market.

TRADING PLAN STEP 6: SET GOALS

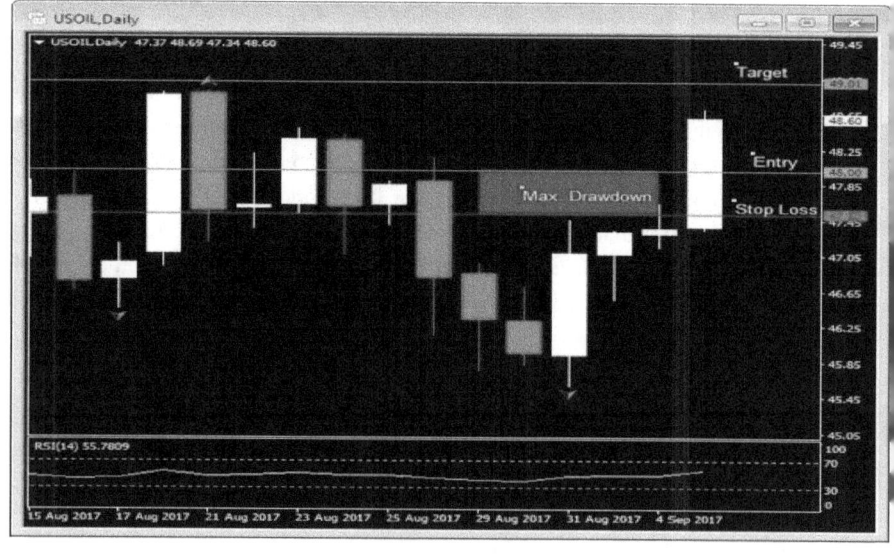

What is the minimum risk/reward that your personality will accept?

- Before entering a trade, set **realistic Targets and Risk/Reward Ratio.**
- **Minimum Risk /Reward Ratio:** More or equal to 1.
- **Set Target Profits:**

    - Daily, weekly and monthly, e.g. "I want to make 20% every month" or "I want to win triple of what I risk for."

    - Example: Goal: "Win Double than Risk"

Risk/Reward: 1:2

The Key Elements of Trading Plan

Enter Long in USOIL at $48.00

Target set at $49.00, i.e. +100pips

Stop loss at $48.50, i.e. -50pips

Now we are almost to open our first trading account. We already know about our daily target and risk. It is the time to divide this our expected profit and risk to each trading position, which we call it here Take profit number and Stop loss number. Never enter in to market without SL and TP. This is the way which we can manage our account and it will be under our control. Just need to mention that setting the SL and TP is not just depend on our risk % and expected profit, we need to check the technical analyze as well.

TRADING PLAN STEP 7: SET EXIT RULES

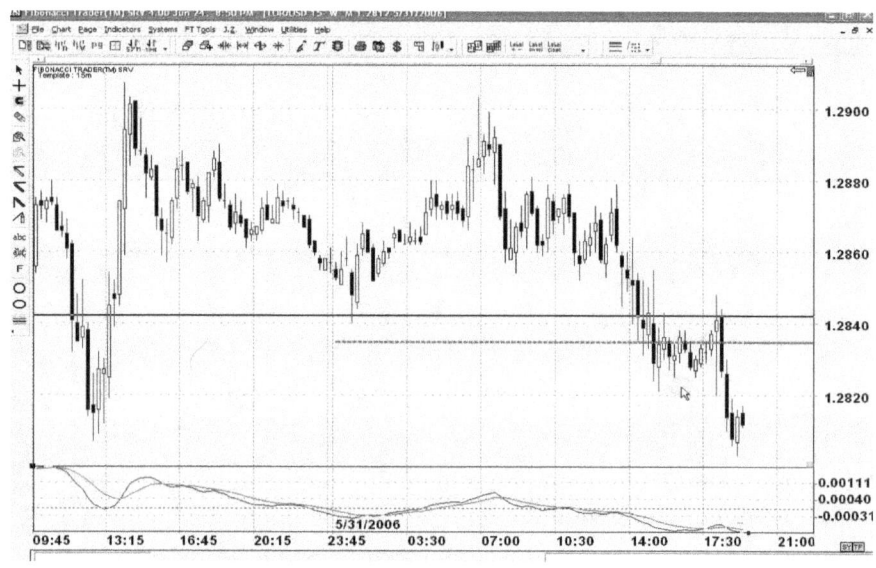

- Set a **Stop Loss** and **Don't Move it!**
- If trend go against you and hits your Stop loss – **Don't worry**
    - Don't take it personal.
    - Majority of traders lose more trades than they win.
    - The important thing is to **manage your overall risk**, **limit your losses** but still **end up** every month **with profit**.
- Always set your stop loss prior entering the trade.

The Key Elements of Trading Plan

- **To break Even: Set a profit target** → If trend gets up to your target, **Sell a portion** → Move stop loss on the rest of your position

    - Remember! – Never risk more than the Risk level % than you have initially set.

Trading is life, we can use our main lessons which we learned in life, here in Trading as well. One of success keys in life is to learn to say NO! Have you ever watched the movie "The Wolf of Wall Street"? There are so many interesting sentences, one of them is: "I don't ask my clients to judge me by my winners, but to judge me by my losers because I have so few -Jordan Belfort of Wolf of Wall Street". You know the reason? As it mentioned above is that most of traders are losing more than what they gain and most reason is again EMOTION, because they want to go against of TREND! They are opening a position and loosing, which is normal and can happen for everybody, but the problem is not that, the problem is that they do that over and over in same time, one after another! Calm down, when you lost and your position had cross the SL, just exit the market, wait, think, check everything and STEP OUT OF THE MARKET! Nothing will happen, no worry! Just say No to your emotion and try to trade in peace, be relax! Never LATE! You have time again to open a position next days or next hours, just think more before doing anything and do not take it personal! We had some rules, just follow them and make sure, as long as you do follow them, you are making money, not 100% profit, but not less than 15% per month, which is the wish for more 80% of traders, because they are losing all their capital, just because of not following the rules and not because they do not know the rules!

TRADING PLAN STEP 8: SET ENTRY RULES

Stop!
Read all the rules

- Exit Rules are more significant
- Set certain Conditions that needs to be achieved in order to take an entry. **Not too many – Keep it simple.**
- *<u>Examples:</u>* "If 50-period Moving average breaks and RSI is not neutral and gives the same direction as MA, then enter the Market."
    - "If Tweezer confirmed with the next Candle, then I will get in"
    - " I'm only interested in Head and shoulders, and triangles"
    - "I only enter new positions between 8:00 – 10:00 in the morning"
- Write down only the opportunities that you identifies and how you will trade them.
- *<u>Important:</u>* <u>don't Chase an entry if you missed it.</u>

Entry rules are as much as important as exit rules! Again, rules are so important,

The Key Elements of Trading Plan

but it does not mean that you are guaranteed, but you what is guaranty? Exactly, FOLLOWING the rules for sure will guaranty your success!

Some of entry rules can be personal, like any time I want to open position, exactly when I am sure what should I do, I will wait 5 more minutes and then will do! Or between "8-10" will not open any position! Or whatever, and some of them are professional rules, like never go against of trend...

TRADING PLAN STEP 9: KEEP RECORDS

No.	Date	Direction	Market	Entry Signal	Target 1	Target 2	Stopped	T1 Hit	T2 Hit	Comment	Base	Quote	PIP count	Risk Reward	Risk Reward Losers
1	08-Aug	Long	NZDUSD	0.7364	0.7380	0.7400	Yes	No		No H1 - SL 0.7330	NZD	USD	-34.00		-2.13
2	08-Aug	Short	NZDUSD	0.7364	0.7305	-	No	Yes		No Daily	NZD	USD	39.00	1.00	
3	10-Aug	Long	EURAUD	1.4867	1.4885	1.4900	No	Yes		Yes H1 - SL 1.4840	EUR	AUD	33.00	1.83	
4	10-Aug	Long	EURAUD	1.4867	1.4940	-	No	Yes		Daily - SL 1.4790	EUR	AUD	73.00	1.00	
5	11-Aug	Short	NZDUSD	0.7282	0.7270	0.7263	Yes	No		No H1 - SL 0.7293	NZD	USD	-12.00		-1.00
6	11-Aug	Short	NZDUSD	0.7282	0.7220	0.7150	No	Yes		No Daily - SL 0.7430	NZD	USD	62.00	1.00	
7	17-Aug	Short	GBPUSD	1.2686	1.2860	1.2840	No	Yes		No H1 - SL 1.2915	GBP	USD	26.00	1.00	
8	18-Aug	Short	GBPAUD	1.6300	1.6270	1.6245	No	Yes		Yes H1 - SL 1.6380	GBP	AUD	55.00	1.83	
9	18-Aug	Short	USDCAD	1.2642	1.2580	1.2540	No	Yes		Yes H4&D - SL 1.2780	USD	CAD	102.00	1.65	
10	21-Aug	Long	EURGBP	0.9133	0.9145	0.9160	No	Yes		Yes H1 - SL 0.9083	EUR	GBP	27.00	2.25	
11	22-Aug	Short	EURJPY	128.60	128.00	-	Yes	No		No H4 - SL 129.30	EUR	JPY	-70.00		-1.17
12	23-Aug	Long	AUDUSD	0.7886	0.7640	-	No	Yes		No Daily - SL 0.7540	AUD	USD	-54.00		-1.17
13	23-Aug	Short	AUDUSD	0.7886	0.7870	-	No	Yes		No H1 - SL 0.7905	AUD	USD	16.00	1.00	
14	23-Aug	Long	AUDNZD	1.0935	1.0980	1.1015	No	Yes		Yes H4&D - SL 1.08635	AUD	NZD	80.00	1.78	
15	25-Aug	Short	EURGBP	0.9206	0.9198	-	Yes	No		No 30M - SL 0.9213	EUR	GBP	-7.00		-0.87
16	25-Aug	Short	EURGBP	0.9206	0.9174	-	Yes	No		No H1 - SL 0.9226	EUR	GBP	-20.00		-0.63
17	29-Aug	Long	GBPJPY	140.85	141.00	141.20	No	Yes		Yes H1 - SL 140.35	GBP	JPY	35.00	2.33	
18	30-Aug	Long	USDJPY	109.96	110.30	110.60	No	Yes		Yes H1&H1 - SL 1.109.30	USD	JPY	64.00	1.88	
19	30-Aug	Long	UK100	7374.50	7406.00	7435.00	No	Yes		Yes H4&D - SL 7345.00	UK1	100	60.50	1.92	
20	31-Aug	Long	NZDJPY	78.92	78.60	78.20	No	Yes		No H4&D - SL 79.50	NZD	JPY	32.00	1.00	
										Total:			527.50	21.48	-6.97

> The understanding on why and how a trade was successful or Not, improves you as a trader
> Keeping good records helps you recognise your mistakes.

Your trading records should contain the following information:

> Targets
> Entry of each trade
> Exit of each trade
> Timeframe
> Support
> Resistance levels
> Daily open range

The Key Elements of Trading Plan

- ➢ Open and Close price of the Day
- ➢ Comments about the trade – Daily and Weekly Review

We are the best teacher of ourselves, as always that we are the best doctor for yourself, as we are our only problem and only solution! Exactly, let me say again that trading is exactly like a life and to achieve the goals here, we need to follow the life rules, here as well. Record everything you did during your weekly trade and it will give you wide view or your acts and market movement. Whenever you will check them you will understand your mistakes first of all and in same time you have the record of market, even in days that you did not trade, but you were following the market and it will help you in your future positions. End of each trading week, sit down and check your record and as third person try to judge yourself and use it as a note that you have as a teacher in class and want to get some points out of that, bold it and tell your students! Let me give you another example out of trading to make it clearer. If you met the people who always taking a note from their daily life and recording everything end of the day, before going to bed, you will understand they are more success than others, why? Because they have a plan for their life and the writing diaries everyday will make their mind to remember everything, their mistakes and their stronger points. Same as trading it will help you to guide your mind and you will understand slowly, slowly that in which markets you are stronger and which one no, which may give you more profit, in which markets you did most mistakes, in which days? Which times and so on. Make sure nobody will be able to help you, more than your daily record and studding that in the end of every trading weeks and months!

RECAP – TIME TO START

- Write it down on a paper if needed.
- Main Rule : **KEEP IT SIMPLE**
- Start your day by **Review your trades** and the **Overall Market Sentiment**.
- Set **Major Resistance and Support levels** for trades triggered you to enter.
- Check if these trades met your conditions
- Always set **stop loss** and **profit target** before entering
- Keep Maximum number of trades and a **fixed Risk level** per day
- Don't set unrealistic targets that probably will become a VERY Realistic loss. . – **Risk management**
- Keep **GREED** away from your trading.
- Accept **LOSS** and stay focused on limiting your losses and learn from your mistakes.
- A Trading Plan cannot guarantee success but a good plan helps you for sure staying in the market – for a New Trader survival is better than failure.

Time to start! If you stay next to swimming pool and read how you have to swim, never will learn it! It is time to go all the steps one after another and make sure you are in right way. Whenever had any mistake, just come back to this book and check where your mistake was, solve it, learn and go ahead. Never scare of making a mistake, it is part of life, part of trade and part of us! As long as you do not have mistaken, you will not learn, if your mistakes are under control and you can review them!

ABOUT THE AUTHOR

- Co-founder and CEO at Ahura Group, which Zero spread is part of that.
- (www.ahuragroup.co)
- Forex Trader since 2011.
- Co-founder and CEO at signal provider company "Zero Spread" from 2017. (www.zerospread.info)

Keep it so simple, life is simple, trading is more!

Ahura Chalki

Aug. 2019

www.ingramcontent.com/pod-product-compliance
Lightning Source LLC
Chambersburg PA
CBHW070945220526
45469CB00007B/2527